THE SHE BEAR

BY

HILLARY DEPIANO

BASED ON THE FAIRY TALE FROM THE TALE OF TALES BY GIAMBATTISTA BASILE

Copyright 2017, 2025 Hillary DePiano
ALL RIGHTS RESERVED

For inquires, requests for permission, to secure rights for performance or other needs, please contact Hillary DePiano through her website at HillaryDePiano.com. **Discounted acting editions are available for schools and groups ordering in bulk for performance or classroom needs.**

CAUTION: Professional and amateurs are hereby warned that this play is fully protected under the copyright laws of the United States of America. All rights, including professional, amateur, motion pictures, recitation, lecturing, public reading, radio broadcasting, television, and the rights of translation into foreign languages are strictly reserved. In its present form, the play is dedicated to the reading public only.

The author controls all rights, including the amateur live stage performance rights,. The right of performance is not transferable.

Copying this play either in print or electronically without written permission of the author is strictly forbidden by law. No part of this publication may be reproduced, copied, stored in a retrieval system, transmitted in any form by any means, electronic, mechanical, photocopying, recording, performing, or otherwise, without written permission of the author.

Due authorship credit must be given on all programs, printing, and advertising for the play.

THE TALE OF TALES PROJECT

Giambattista Basile (1566–1632) wrote and compiled the 60 fairy tales within *The Pentamerone* (*Lo cunto de li cunti* in Neapolitan or *The Tale of Tales* in English) in Naples, Italy in the early 1600s. His sister, Adriana, published it in two volumes in 1634 and 1636 after his death. While not widely known, it's important historically because the Brothers Grimm later used it as the source for their far more famous fairy tale collection. *The Tale of Tales* contains the earliest known versions of fairy tales such as Sleeping Beauty, Cinderella, Rapunzel, Puss in Boots, Hansel and Gretel and more.

But I'm not interested in the stories everyone has heard of. I like the obscure ones, the weird ones lost to time. Why do we obsessively retell the same dozen fairy tales when there are plenty of other great ones we ignore?

It bothers me. So, since early 2013, I've been adapting these lesser-known tales for modern audiences to bring these stories back into circulation. I've modernized them with today's audiences in mind while still staying true to the spirit of the originals. Wherever possible, I also preserved the names from the original fairy tale and, where characters were unnamed, I've named them within the historical context and often with names from elsewhere in the Tales themselves.

This project is still ongoing. For the latest list of all the tales I've adapted from The Tale of Tales and what I'm working on next, visit HillaryDePiano.com.

BIBLIOGRAPHY

Basile, Giambattista (2007). Giambattista Basile's "The Tale of Tales, or Entertainment for Little Ones". Translated by Nancy L. Canepa, illustrated by Carmelo Lettere, foreword by Jack Zipes. Detroit, MI: Wayne State University Press. ISBN 978-0-8143-2866-8.

Standalone One-Acts
There are standalone one-act versions of every fairy tale I've adapted from *The Tale of Tales*.

The Myrtle
35-45 minutes, 5 m 8 f (6-20+ performers possible)
A prince discovers his myrtle tree turns into a fairy maiden at sundown.

Goosed!
(based on The Goose)
35-45 minutes, 2 m 6 f 8 any (11-20+ performers possible)
Two poor sisters rescue a golden goose but their sneaky neighbors want it for themselves.

Arm Candy
(based on Pintosmalto)
45-60 minutes, 2 m, 4 f (5-7+ performers possible)
When a brilliant inventor builds the perfect husband out of sugar, he's stolen by a queen who wants him for herself.

The Fourth Orange
(based on The Merchant with characters from Carlo Gozzi's The Love of Three Oranges)
25-35 minutes, 4 m, 6 f, 5 any (7-20+ actors possible)
There were only supposed to be three oranges but Franceschina had to stick her nose where it didn't belong.

The She Bear
30-45 minutes, 2 m 2 f (4-10+ performers possible)
Is the prince losing his mind or has he really fallen in love with a bear?

VARDIELLO
10-15 minutes, 1 m, 1 f, 2 any
How much damage can one half-wit do before his mother gives him the boot? (Now published exclusively through Brooklyn Publishers!)

~

Want to combine plays to make an evening's entertainment?
You'll find shortened versions of the most popular fairy tales in this fun and fantastical full length!

THE FOURTH ORANGE
AND OTHER FAIRY TALES YOU'VE NEVER EVEN HEARD OF
100-120 minutes, 25w 12m 11any (11 to 60+ performers possible)
It's bedtime bedlam when a washed-up clown tries to sell three unruly princesses on something other than their fairy tale favorites.

Looking for something even more flexible?
Mix and match the tales above to create an evening's entertainment and I'll provide interstitial material and opening and closing scenes to connect the tales together no matter what combination you choose!

FOR MORE INFORMATION ABOUT THIS CUSTOM OPTION, [EMAIL HILLARY DEPIANO AT HILLARY@HILLARYDEPIANO.COM](mailto:hillary@hillarydepiano.com).

The She Bear

The She Bear premiered on April 26, 2018 at The Annie Wright Schools in Tacoma, WA with the following cast and crew.

```
PRINCE .................................................................Caroline Hall
PREZIOSA (BEAR) ............................................... Bea Hunt
QUEEN ..................................................................Dana Hicks
TRUFFALDINO...................................................Elodie Soustelle
ANDREA ..............................................................Rae Wartelle
WOLF ...................................................................Emily Leise
GUARD ................................................................Emily Leise
```

Director
Elizabeth Gettel

Assistant Director/Stage Manager
Maddie Strate

Set and Light Design
Scott Campbell

Costume Director
Terah Gruber

Costumes
Xiomara Choto- Mueller, Emily Simons, Emily Mullencamp, Calire Noh

Wig Designer
Xiomara Choto-Mueller

Stage Crew
Pearl Brooke, Jack Montgomery, Isabella Smith, Elodie Soustelle, Leo Howard, Rae Wartelle

Construction Support
Katty Sun and Theatre 360

Program Design
Lauren Christenson

PRODUCTION NOTES

IMPROVISATION

In the spirit of the slapstick of classic Italian theatre and commedia dell'arte tradition that inspired these adaptations, you're encouraged to put your own spin on all comedic bits and fights and to explore the physical comedy through improvisation. If you can come up with something funnier than the stage directions describe, go for it! I'm even happy to approve changes in dialog or more modern references, just run it by me first. For performer safety, avoid injury by always making sure you finalize all physical routines before the show opens. While you certainly don't have to, you're welcome to perform the show in masked commedia style if desired.

CONTENT

While this fairy tale is PG as written (as most classic fairy tales are), I'm happy to work with schools and other groups who may need to tone it down to be able to perform it. Be it language or situational, please email me (hillary@hillarydepiano.com) with any issues you run into. I'll do my best to help you find a workaround.

CASTING NOTES

I encourage blind casting in all cases where it comes to race, gender, body type, etc. If you're in a casting pickle, please email me to explain your casting needs and I'll help you out. I can give you alternate character names and lines or grant permission to change character genders as needed, whatever we need to do to make it happen.

STAGING

Staging for this play can be as simple or as complicated as you want it to be. Because of the storybook nature of the tales, costumes can be anything from elaborate period pieces to paper bag tunics with just a few elements to suggest the character. Sets can be elaborately illustrated pages from a picture book, the crayon drawings of a child's imagination or a few furniture pieces where the audience's imagination does the rest.

INCREASING OR DECREASING CAST SIZE

Need more roles? The ensemble of wolves and guards can be as large as you need to accommodate your performers.

Please don't hesitate to contact me (hillary@hillarydepiano.com) for any reason. I'm here to help!

The She Bear at The Annie Wright Schools in Tacoma, WA

CHARACTERS
(In order of appearance)

PRINCE CIENZO, the prince of Running Water

ANDREA, a royal guard and the prince's best friend

THE SHE-BEAR, a bear with a strangely human nature

QUEEN ANTONELLA, Queen of Running Water, Cienzo's mother

WOLVES

GUARDS

SETTING
A fairytale kingdom.

TIME
The imaginary past.

THE SHE BEAR
SCENE 1

(A dark forest.)

(Prince Cienzo, armed with a spear, checks the ground for signs of the bear. The guard, Andrea, follows.)

PRINCE CIENZO
Ah ha! Fresh tracks! It's been this way. Where are the others? Oh, hang them if they can't keep up. Come on then, Andrea, before it gets too far ahead!

ANDREA
Wait, your majesty.

PRINCE CIENZO
Don't tell me you've lost your breath already! I expect those clods to have trouble keeping up with my stride, but you're my best man.

ANDREA
It's just... We're at the very edge of the kingdom out here. If it's crossed over to Dry Mountain, we may as well give it up.

PRINCE CIENZO
Give it up? We've barely been out here a fortnight, and you want me to trot back home to my mother? No, friend. If I'm going home, it's with that blasted bear's hide on my saddle all sharpened teeth and claws. You remember the boar? The Queen fret over those bloodstained tusks for weeks. If this bear's as big as they say, it could buy me whole months of sweet freedom!

ANDREA
I'm still not convinced there's a bear at all.

PRINCE CIENZO
That farmer seemed sure enough when he sent for us.

ANDREA

Aye, but he also stank of drink and twice referred to that goat as his sister.

PRINCE CIENZO

You can't deny there was a likeness between them. Besides, more's the better if there is no bear. We can pretend to hunt it as long as we like and only go back when we grow sick of it! It's not a bad life in these woods, where a man can live by his own laws, no one trying chain you up.

ANDREA

If you say so. A few days of this dark forest is plenty to remind me of the pleasures of the court, especially this trip coming so soon after the last two. I love the thrill of the hunting dance as much as anyone, but I'd still rather take a twirl with one of those pretty princess of yours. Certainly a nicer place to stick your spear, if you catch my meaning.

PRINCE CIENZO

You'd think that, but it's a trap. Love is the bait of a snare and only a madman would let it snag them. All it takes is for one to catch my eye and the Queen will lock me up in marriage plans before I can blink. My parents screamed at each other my whole life until my father finally died just so he could have the satisfaction of the last word. No, friend. I'd be a fool to sign up for that misery.

ANDREA

There's plenty that seem to like it well enough.

PRINCE CIENZO

Hmph.

ANDREA

And... those that do would rather be home with their mates on a cold night like this than chasing an imaginary bear around the woods.

PRINCE CIENZO

But the tracks!

ANDREA
Forgive me, Prince Cienzo, but with as little light as there is at this hour I'm not sure those are even bear tracks. We've been through this twisted maze of trees so many times, they might even be yours for all we know.

PRINCE CIENZO
Oh, for heaven's sake. I had a feeling they'd put you up to something like this, what with all the grumbles and dragging feet. Fine. Go! Tell the men they've won. We'll give up the chase and head back for home at daybreak.

ANDREA
They will be very grateful.

PRINCE CIENZO
Spare me your scraping. I should have all your heads. I hope you'll all at least think of me as I'm wooed into an early grave for your comfort.

ANDREA
I suspect you'll manage, sir.

PRINCE CIENZO
Just go. Get that smug grin out of my sight.

(Andrea bows slightly and exits)

My prints indeed. That one's not my print. It looks like an overgrown dog.

(A howl)

What was that? Andrea? Are you still there?

(Additional howls)

Wolves?

(A pack of wolves come stalking out of the woods, snarling around their sharp teeth. If needed, it can be a single large wolf.. The prince raises his spear.)

Keep back, beasts! I may be alone, but I've been party to enough hunts to know-- aah!

> *(They launch themselves at him. He manages to injure one with his spear but another bites his leg. He screams as he falls to the ground, losing his weapon. They are all on him now, biting and clawing in a snarling mass. The prince kicks and flails, but all he can do is scream in pain as they tear at him.)*

Aargh! Andrea! Help me, someone!

> *(A roar fills the air. The wolves all stop and look to the sound. There's another roar as a massive She-Bear comes lumbering out of the woods and rises up on her hind legs.)*

By the gods...

> *(The prince can only watch as the wolves all growl at the She-Bear. The bear advances and swats the nearest one away as if it's nothing. The other wolves launch themselves at her. One tears at her underside while another gnaws at her legs. One manages to leap up onto her back. They bring her down, and she roars with pain. It seems like they've beaten her. The prince realizes now is his chance to get away. He tries to rise, but as soon as he puts weight on his leg, he lets out a sound of pain and falls back to the ground.)*

Ugh! Blast it!

> *(The sound distracts the wolves. It's all the chance the bear needs. She tosses them all off, slamming them into trees and ground with a crunch of bones and startled yelps. The wolves that survive this attack tuck their tails and limp away as fast as they can while the bear raises herself to her full height and roars with triumph at their*

> *retreat. The prince is trying to drag himself to his spear, but his injuries are too great and the pain is immense.)*

If I could only reach my spear I...

> *(Just as he reaches it, he realizes the bear is right above him. He raises the weapon.)*

Keep your distance, beast, or...

> *(They regard each other for a moment. The bear doesn't move. The prince lowers the spear.)*

...you weren't... you saved me. I called for help and you... I must not be thinking clearly. I've lost so much blood but... Your eyes they're... different.

> *(With a snuff, the bear turns to go. She's moving gingerly, dragging an injured leg while one paw holds at a gash across her stomach.)*

Wait! Don't go. It's OK. Here... See?

> *(He tosses the spear away and holds up his hands. The bear pauses and looks back at him.)*

Listen to me. Your fur is dark with blood and that gash across your middle... it's too deep. You'll bleed to death out here even if the wolves don't come back for you, which they will, as soon as they realize how badly you're hurt and... By the gods, I must have hit my head harder than I thought. I'm talking to a bear like it can speak human.

> *(The bear regards him. She makes a small snuff.)*

...but you do understand, don't you? I can see it in your eyes and I don't know how or why but... I cannot let you crawl back into the woods to die, not after what you've done for me today. Back at the palace, there are doctors, they can't refuse me if I tell them to fix you and--

> *(Sound from offstage. The prince's men*

have come for him at last. The bear starts to run.)

It's OK! Those are my men. They're coming for me. Please... You'll die out here. Let me take you with us. It's just until you're well and then I'll bring you right back. I give you my word.

(The bear looks from him to the woods and back again. She makes an indecisive whine.)

You saved my life. Please, let me save yours. It's the least I can do.

(With shouts of "There he is!" and "It's the prince!" Andrea and the rest of the hunting party enter. Their chatter stops as they see the bear.)

ANDREA

It's massive! A monster!

(They raise their weapons. The bear is ready to flee again.)

PRINCE CIENZO

No! Lower your weapons! I command you! I will have the head of any man that harms this animal, so help me I will.

(They look to each other and Andrea slowly lowers his weapon. The others follow suit.)

ANDREA

Your majesty? What happened here?

PRINCE CIENZO

There will be time enough for stories on the ride home. For now, we need bandages and the cart for the bear. It's coming back with us.

ANDREA

It is? Are you sure that's...

PRINCE CIENZO
How do you think the Queen will react when she hears that you let her only son bleed to death on the dirt because you wanted to play at questions? The bear is coming. That is final.

ANDREA
I... I'm sorry, your majesty. Whatever your command, we'll make it happen. Let me help you back to camp. Gods, but you're in poor shape. We must get you back to the court. We should have the cart ready for our... guest within an hour and be on our way.

(He helps the prince to his feet and starts taking him off. The prince stops and looks back at the bear.)

PRINCE CIENZO
Come along, bear. Let's get us both patched up.

(The bear stares after him. She glances back at the woods. Then she lets out a long, very human, sigh and limps gingerly after the prince. All exit.)

SCENE 2

(A walled garden in the center of the palace, several weeks later.)

(The She-Bear shuffles restlessly around the enclosure. Offstage, lights and sounds of a ball in progress. The prince sneaks in a moment later, dressed for the ball.)

PRINCE CIENZO
Pst! It's me!

(The bear turns.)

Over here where they won't see us from the ballroom.

(The bear lumbers over to where he is.)

I pleaded sour stomach so hopefully they won't notice I'm gone for a bit.

(She growls.)

It is not a lie! Not really. The whole thing really does make me want to vomit.

(She snorts.)

Anyway, I'm sorry it's been so long since I was able to steal away for a visit. As soon as I was back up on my feet, my mother's been determined to keep me that way. Balls this, dinners that. Rows and rows of princesses and all of them as interesting as blades of grass. How I missed these moments with you, bear. Those girls fill up every second with prattle when you say so much more with a small snuff or growl. Whenever you and I sit like this we don't even need words, we understand each other perfectly.

(The bear snuffs. Companionable silence for a moment.)

I'll let you in on a little secret, bear. Watch this.

(He walks around her.)

See? The leg's totally mended. I've been faking the limp for weeks now. It spares me from the dancing which is the worst part anyway.

(She snorts again. A light waltz plays from the ball.)

Oh, sure, scoff at my pain. You don't know what it's like to be dragged around a dance floor worrying about where to put your feet and exactly how much eye contact is appropriate when all you want is to go sit somewhere where everyone isn't staring at you. Here, I'll show you... do you dance, bear?

(The bear growls.)

No, no. Not that cheap circus stuff, I mean... Here. I'll show you. Give me your paw, m'lady.

(She reluctantly gives him her paw and he starts to lead her in a waltz. She shuffles awkwardly.)

Just move your feet like... No it's more like... Hmm... Well, I suppose this was foolish of me. I just thought... Forgive me, friend, but sometimes it's hard to remember you're only an animal.

> *(She growls. She gives into the music then, waltzing like a human girl.)*

Ha! Who'd have thought? You're as light on your paws as any of those puff pastries.

> *(They waltz around the garden. The prince laughs.)*

Gods help me, I'm actually enjoying this. Oh, bear. Everything is so much easier with you. If it were like this with those girls upstairs, it would be so different.

> *(He twirls her. She's really into it now and goes into the move with flourish.)*

You dance like you've been doing it since you were a child. Are you secretly royalty, bear?

> *(The bear stops cold.)*

I was only joking I... Mother?

> *(The Queen steps out of the shadows. She's been watching them. The bear goes back to all fours, acting more like a bear and less human.)*

QUEEN ANTONELLA
I knew I'd find you here. For heaven's sake, Cienzo! Have you taken leave of your senses? You're the sole heir to the throne!

PRINCE CIENZO
That I am, which means I can do what I like, no matter how little you approve.

QUEEN ANTONELLA
Get away from it! It's a wild animal! A mindless beast that could tear you in half.

PRINCE CIENZO
Mother...

(He doesn't move but the bear lumbers away from him with a snuff.)

QUEEN ANTONELLA
There was that story not three years ago of a bear that charged into the King of Dry Mountain's wedding, rampaging through the castle and terrifying the guests. His young bride was never seen again, probably food for the bear's belly. Their lands aren't all that far from where you hunt, how do you know this isn't that very same murderous bear?

PRINCE CIENZO
Because if she wanted to eat me, it would have been easy enough in the woods that day and instead she saved my life. Besides, the way I heard it, the King of Dry Rock was trying to marry his own daughter not a day after he buried her mother so who are we to say that bear didn't do the poor girl a favor?

QUEEN ANTONELLA
Oh, you're awful. And you'll just keep carrying on and sneaking in to cavort with your ridiculous pet no matter how often I command you to stay away.

(The bear growls softly.)

PRINCE CIENZO
And how often have I told you I don't want to marry? And yet you keep parading princesses down my throat.

QUEEN ANTONELLA
What would those fine families up there think if they saw you carrying on like this? You look utterly ridiculous! They'll think you mad! For that matter, I think you mad when I see you twirling around with that monster. And all this while, you've said you were still too lame to dance. When I think of the slight if they find your feet are sturdy enough when it suits you.

PRINCE CIENZO

What do I care for any of them? I'd sooner marry this bear. Tell them that. Maybe it'll get them all off my back if they think I'm out of my mind and in love with a bear. Right, buddy?

(He goes to tussle the bear's fur but she growls and moves farther away.)

QUEEN ANTONELLA

This is all a joke to you, isn't it? Well someday soon I will be dead and then, like it or not, you will be King. Forgive me if I'm not willing to indulge your selfish whims when the future of the entire Kingdom and everything your father and I worked for is at stake.

PRINCE CIENZO

I... I wasn't thinking. I'm sorry, mother.

QUEEN ANTONELLA

My dear, sweet boy. I know what it's like to reconcile duties and desires. But I promise you, there is someone out there that can serve for both.

PRINCE CIENZO

Ha!

QUEEN ANTONELLA

You'll see in time that I'm right. But you'll never find that someone if you insist on hiding from the possibility.

PRINCE CIENZO

I suppose...

QUEEN ANTONELLA

But, for heaven's sake, leave this poor beast out of it. The doctors declared it sound weeks ago but you've always got some excuse why we can't send it back to its home in the forest.

(With a small sound of pain, the bear glares at the prince.)

####PRINCE CIENZO
I thought it was better to be safe, make sure everything was really, truly healed before...

####QUEEN ANTONELLA
It's an animal. It's not meant to live caged like this. He's been a good friend to you, this bear, but it's time to let him go.

####PRINCE CIENZO
She.

####QUEEN ANTONELLA
What's that?

####PRINCE CIENZO
You said "he." That's a She-Bear. But you're right about the rest. I did make a promise. I'll... I'll make the arrangements. She should go home.

####QUEEN ANTONELLA
It's for the best. Now, come. Let's return to our guests. You're even spared of dancing... until the next one anyway.

####PRINCE CIENZO
I figured I couldn't keep that ruse up forever.

(He exits. The Queen starts to follow but stops and she and the bear regard each other from opposite sides of the garden.)

####QUEEN ANTONELLA
I understand why he spends so much time in here. It really is like it can understand what we're saying. But, tame or not, I'll be glad when we're rid of it.

(She starts to leave. The bear growls.)
Have something to say about that, have you, bear? Eager to go back to your home?

(The bear growls again)
...or is it the opposite?

(The bear snorts.)

Interesting. I've heard it said that you should never get between a mother bear and her cub and I think you'll find the same could be said of a Queen.

(The bear growls softly.)

We understand each other, don't we, beast?

(She exits. The bear paces the enclosure, making small indecisive sounds.)

SCENE 3

(The prince's bedroom in the middle of the night.)

(The prince lies in bed, tossing and turning. He finally gives up, rising to pace the patch of moonlight on the floor.)

PRINCE CIENZO

It's no use. I can't sleep with my mind racing like this. And I know it's a crazy thought, not even worth entertaining, but now that it's entered my head it's spreading like fire until I can think of nothing else. It all started with a joke and now... My mother speaks true, it's not right to keep a wild thing caged, but... but it's madness to even think it, isn't it? Men do not fall in love with bears! And yet, I can think of nothing but the gaping hole that will be left in my heart when the She-Bear is gone. It's not the bear, not claws and fur, that I need like the air itself, it's the soul that... But are these not more ravings? Because what soul does a bear have but a bear's soul? I'm no longer making sense even to my own ears. Gods, what if I really have taken leave of my senses?

(He goes to the window that overlooks the bear's garden.)

Blast it, bear! The only creature in the world whose advice I need right now and... where is she? She usually beds down just over--

(He gasps as he catches sight of a beautiful princess dressed as if for her wedding. She sits in on a bench in the bear's garden softly weeping in the moonlight.)

Wha--? You! You there!

(The princess startles and runs away.)

No! Please, stop! Wait!

(He rushes out of his rooms and tears all the way down to the garden, still in his bed clothes.)

SCENE 4

(The day turns to night. The Queen enters.)

QUEEN ANTONELLA

There you are! The whole castle's been in uproar, the procession was supposed to leave a quarter of an hour ago and--

(The bear snorts at her. The Queen goes to the Prince. The bear paces the garden.)

Have you been out here all night in just your bed clothes? You're shivering like you've got the very chill of death in you. Come, let's go inside and get you warm. Cienzo? Answer me. Answer your mother.

(The prince doesn't acknowledge her. He continues muttering to himself and staring vacantly.)

It's like he's snapped. Broken and out of his head. Guards! Someone, fetch the physicians! The prince has gone mad!

(Andrea and the guards come tearing in. All this activity upsets the prince who covers his ears and starts mumbling louder.)

ANDREA
The doctor is on the way, your majesty.

PRINCE CIENZO
...the bear is the bear is the bear...

QUEEN ANTONELLA
What's that?

PRINCE CIENZO
...is the bear is the bear is the bear...

QUEEN ANTONELLA
I knew it!

ANDREA
Your grace?

QUEEN ANTONELLA
He said, "It's the bear." You heard my son, clear as day. It's that monster that's done this to him.

ANDREA
I--

(The bear growls and tries to go to the prince's side.)

QUEEN ANTONELLA
Guards! Don't let that thing near my son. I don't know what you did to him, beast, but you stay away! You there, take the prince in, get him warm.

(They start to move the prince inside. The bear follows but the guards don't let her pass. The bear growls and rises to her full height. The Queen takes a step back and the guards target the bear with their weapons.)

It's attacking! That's it! Andrea, it's time you and your men did what you should have done in the first place. Kill the bear. I want it destroyed for what it did to my son.

ANDREA
But--

QUEEN ANTONELLA
I want it dead. That's an order.

(The Queen follows the prince out. The guards attempt to restrain the bear as she lets out a terrible pained roar.)

SCENE 5

(The Prince's bedroom.)

(Prince Cienzo lies in bed, feverish, sleeping fitfully and talking in his sleep. His mother sits by his side, dabbing at his head with a cloth.)

PRINCE CIENZO
The bear... the girl... the bear!

(He wakes with a gasp, startling the Queen who sits by his side.)
Where am I?

QUEEN ANTONELLA
At last! You've been ill for so long they said you might never wake again but I knew my boy was stronger than that.

PRINCE CIENZO
Mother?

QUEEN ANTONELLA
Yes! You're thinking clearly again. Your mind was clouded with some kind of fever madness.

PRINCE CIENZO
I remember. There was... a girl... and the bear... and I thought... Uhn.

(He tries to rise but end up falling back clutching his head and moaning in pain.)

QUEEN ANTONELLA
Shh! Lie back, dear. It's alright. There's nothing to worry about. You're safe. The bear cannot get you now. I had Andrea destroy that awful thing.

PRINCE CIENZO
No! No, it cannot be--

(tries to rise again)

QUEEN ANTONELLA
Be still. Don't get up! Nurse! Guards! Shh, the doctors will have something to help calm you down, you'll see. Blast it, where is everyone?

(The prince struggles against her)

PRINCE CIENZO
Where is she? Let me go!

(Andrea runs in)

ANDREA
Your majesty? I heard a shout and...

PRINCE CIENZO
My poor bear! Is it true?

QUEEN ANTONELLA
Andrea. He's hysterical and I don't have the strength to restrain him. Keep him in bed. I must find the doctors, get him some kind of sedative.

(She exits. The prince turns on Andrea.)

PRINCE CIENZO
You! What did you do to her, villain?

ANDREA
Uh, your highness, perhaps it's best if--

PRINCE CIENZO

(The prince lunges at Andrea but the guard evades.)
You did it. You killed her. I'll have you stuffed and mounted on my wall like the beast you are!

ANDREA
Cienzo! Wait, please, old friend! I can explain.

PRINCE CIENZO
There is nothing I want to hear from any man monster enough to raise his weapons to that sweet bear.

(He attacks Andrea. The prince is weakened but his friend doesn't want to hurt him.)

ANDREA
The bear is alive! Please, you must listen to me! The queen ordered me to kill the She-Bear, that is true. But I couldn't do the deed. I know what the creature meant to you and even if she did somehow cause your madness and your mind was gone for good I couldn't--

PRINCE CIENZO
Is that what they say about me? That I'm out of my mind.

ANDREA
Uh, well, there was talk but--

PRINCE CIENZO
It's no matter. So, where is she then?

ANDREA
We took her back to her forest where the Queen's rage can never reach her again. She's safe, your highness, and free.

PRINCE CIENZO
What? She'll think that I... No. No this will not do at all.

(he starts trying to put clothes on over his nightgown)

ANDREA
Wait! Where are you doing?

PRINCE CIENZO
I am going to find her. I must speak with her and understand if what I saw that night was magic or madness.

ANDREA
You're not going anywhere! You have been ill for weeks! You're weak and barely recovered.

(He bars the door)

PRINCE CIENZO
Step aside, friend.

ANDREA
No. I have governed my tongue all this time but this is too much. You were at death's door and at the first sign of recovery you're babbling about running off into the woods and for what? To talk to a bear? What kind of conversation do you think you can have when one side is only growls and grunts?

PRINCE CIENZO
So there is it. Even you think I'm crazy.

ANDREA
How can I not? I've grown fond of the beast too in her time here but, tame though she may be, she's still just an animal. A dumb animal the likes of which I've killed dozens of in your company.

PRINCE CIENZO
These days I find I've lost my taste for the sport.

ANDREA
And while the fever may have broken, there's nothing you've said

yet today that hasn't sounded like more ravings. You must get back into bed and get well. Then you'll see that I'm doing you a kindness by not letting you go.

PRINCE CIENZO
Is that so?

ANDREA
I'm sorry.

PRINCE CIENZO
Well, then I suppose you're right. Better than I just lay back down here in bed and let them drug me up to my eyeballs.

ANDREA
Well, um, yes, I suppose...

PRINCE CIENZO
Back to bed I go. Fluff my pillows for me, won't you, Andrea?

ANDREA
Uh, certainly.

(Andrea moves towards the bed. The prince takes his chance and shoves the bed over, trapping Andrea.)

Ugh!

PRINCE CIENZO
Goodbye, Andrea. Hope my mother doesn't kill you for this.

(He grabs a jacket and runs out of the room. Andrea struggles to get free.)

ANDREA
Wait! Your highness! Damn it!

(He gets free a moment later and tears out after the prince.)

SCENE 6

(A few days later. The Queen paces in the garden. Andrea enters.)

QUEEN ANTONELLA
Andrea. At last. Your scout said there was news of my son?

ANDREA
There is news, your grace, but nothing good. We found his horse on the first day, half starved and wandering. What little supplies he had were still in the saddle bag. The men and I rode all over those woods but I'm afraid--

QUEEN ANTONELLA
No. I will believe Cienzo is dead when I stand before his body. The prince is out there. You will continue searching. This is on you, Andrea. If you'd obeyed my order to kill the beast or at least had the sense not to tell him you'd left it alive, the prince would still be here.

ANDREA
Your majesty, you cannot possibly blame me more than I blame myself. If I had just humored him, I could have set out with him then at least I'd--

QUEEN ANTONELLA
What's that?

(There is commotion offstage.)

ANDREA
Can it be? Queen Antonella! It's the prince!

QUEEN ANTONELLA
Oh...

(The Queen is left speechless as the bear ambles into the garden carrying the barely conscious prince. He's in poor shape. His bedclothes and the coat he tossed over it

are filthy and torn. The bear lays the prince gently on the bench. The prince stirs fitfully and the Queen runs to him.)

My son! Cienzo! He lives! He's half crazed from hunger. Someone fetch him some food and water.

(Andrea runs out)

Oh, my dear, sweet boy! We feared the worst! All the guards in the kingdom could not find you and yet, Mr. Bear over here proves your savior yet again.

(the bear snorts. Andrea has returned with a tray of food and drink.)

ANDREA

I believe it is a She-Bear, your majesty.

PRINCE CIENZO

The bear...

QUEEN ANTONELLA

Here. You must eat something. Your wandering has made your illness so much worse and you must restore some of your strength.

(The Queen tries to feed him but he refuses)
Come on, open up! He's refusing it. Andrea, you give it a try.

ANDREA

It's me, old friend. Andrea. Come on, now. You've got to eat something.

(The prince refuses the food)
He won't take it, your majesty.

QUEEN ANTONELLA

You won't eat for your best mate, your own mother? Then who?

PRINCE CIENZO

...the bear...

QUEEN ANTONELLA

Oh, for goodness sake, you want the bear to feed you? That's utterly ridiculous and I refuse to...

> *(The prince turns away from her. The Queen looks at the bear)*

Fine. I give up. I only want you happy and whole, after all, who cares what it takes to get you there. Let the bear be your nurse for all I care if it makes you well again.

> *(She steps away from the prince and gestures to the bear. The bear takes her place next to the prince. She tries to pour him a cup of tea but her paws are too large and she struggles, knocking food and cups over, trying to right them. She gets frustrated and lets out a roar, ready to flip the table.)*

Bear...

> *(The bear whips growls but stops as she sees the expression on the Queen's face.)*

It's alright. You can do it. Just try it again. Nice and slow.

> *(The bear takes a deep breath and begins again, slower. She manages to get her paw awkwardly around the tea pot and pour the prince a cup. She cradles the prince's head and gets some of the liquid into his mouth. He doesn't fight it.)*

That's it. You've got it. Nice and easy.

> *(With a tiny knife and fork dwarfed in her massive paws, the bear cuts bits of food and feeds them gingerly to the prince . The prince eats and gradually regains his color until at last he is conscious.)*

ANDREA

He's coming around.

QUEEN ANTONELLA

Remarkable!

PRINCE CIENZO
(groggily) Wha? Where... Dearest bear! I was looking for you.

(She nuzzles him affectionately.)
And mother? Where am I?

QUEEN ANTONELLA
You're home, saved again by your She-Bear. Forgive me, bear. I have been wrong about you. You really do care for my son in a way that is startlingly human.

PRINCE CIENZO
That's why I needed to find her. What I needed to tell you, bear. I had to make sure you knew that even if it doesn't make a bit of sense... I love you.

(The She-Bear moves away with a small whimper.)

ANDREA
Hoo, boy.

QUEEN ANTONELLA
I thought as much. I admit it will take some time for me to get used to the idea but I'm through fighting it. What are matters of secession compared with matters of the heart? All I want is for my son to be happy and whole. If being with the bear is what that takes, then that is enough for me.

PRINCE CIENZO
Bear?

(The bear is poised at the edge of the garden, ready to flee.)
I would know your heart. Are my feelings returned?

(She hesitates and then nods. Yes.)
But it is not enough. You would still flee from me? Even though I can see it breaks your heart as much as it does mine?

(She looks from him to her escape with a miserable whine)

QUEEN ANTONELLA

You can't expect a wild thing to live between walls, not when even you chafe at them.

PRINCE CIENZO

Then I shall go with her. I will renounce my title, my whole life, if it means we'll never have to part again.

(The bear turns back to him, surprised. The prince struggles to his feet.)

All this time I thought love was a kind of madness. But now I realize... that's just how it looks from the outside. When you're in love, that's when everything finally makes sense. If it's a trap, it's one I walk into willingly. Whether we're surrounded by trees or turrets, bear, as long as I'm with you, I'm home.

(The bear watches him for the moment. Then she rises to her fall height and runs to the prince so quickly Andrea reaches for his weapon.)

ANDREA

Watch out, your highness, she's--

(The Queen puts out a hand to stop him)

QUEEN ANTONELLA

Wait, Andrea. It's alright.

(The bear launches herself into the prince's arms and they kiss.)

ANDREA

Wow, they're really going at it.

QUEEN ANTONELLA

Hmm. Yes, this will certainly take some getting used to.

(The prince pulls back, taking a small stick from his mouth)

PRINCE CIENZO

What's this? A stick?

(With a blast of magic, the bear transforms into Princess Preziosa)

QUEEN ANTONELLA

What sorcery is this?

ANDREA

Whoa!

PREZIOSA

Oh, no! The stick... I must get it back under my tongue at once or--

PRINCE CIENZO

You! You're the girl I saw that night!

PREZIOSA

No! I mean, yes, but... Oh, I cannot be here, I should never have come... He'll find me. Please, give me back my stick so that I may go back to hiding in the forest.

QUEEN ANTONELLA

Dear girl, who are you? Who are you hiding from?

PREZIOSA

I am Princess Preziosa of Dry Mountain. My mother was gone and my father... He threatened to kill me if I refused but to even think of it! I was trapped between a terrible marriage and death and all I could do was pray for escape. A fairy took pity on a miserable girl and gave me that enchantment but all it did was transform me into a monster. So I ran. I ran and I hid and let the beast take over or my grief would eat me whole. I didn't think I had any humanity left until that moment I saw you in the forest. But, oh, I never should have followed you. Don't you see? If I'm not hidden under fur, he'll find me, he'll force me to...

(She cries. The Prince takes her into his arms.)

PRINCE CIENZO
Princess Preziosa, anyone who dares harm you will face my steel.

ANDREA
Mine as well.

QUEEN ANTONELLA
And my... well, my guards' steel anyway. You poor thing. No one should have to endure what you have been through. You are under our protection now and the Kingdom of Running Water can be your sanctuary for as long as you need it.

PREZIOSA
But my father...

QUEEN ANTONELLA
Wouldn't dare. Our army is twice his.

PRINCE CIENZO
You are safe at last.

PREZIOSA
It's strange. I thought Preziosa was buried forever, a ghost wedged inside the soul of a bear, and that was all the protection she would ever find. All this time, I never thought I could feel safe as myself again. And yet...

PRINCE CIENZO
You have been very brave, princess.

PREZIOSA
I ran. I hid. Without my teeth and claws, I'm just a girl.

QUEEN ANTONELLA
But you kept your humanity even though the world has never been anything but wild and savage to you. It's easy to discount how much strength it takes to hold onto yourself instead of giving into our baser, animal natures. And yet, even as a beast, you were a

better person than the King of Dry Mountain could ever hope to be.

PRINCE CIENZO
Princess, I know what it feels like to almost lose yourself. Bear or girl, princess or beast, the core of you bound itself to the very core of me and pulled me back up into the light. You saved me.

PREZIOSA
And now you have saved me, my lord. It seems like all we've done since we met is save each other's lives. Will we ever not be in each other's debt?

QUEEN ANTONELLA
No. I'm afraid that's what love is. It's saving each other, every day, from the brink just by being there. Even though Cienzo's father could be a real bear, no offense, he was the one solid thing in a sea of uncertainty and I miss him every single day.

PRINCE CIENZO
You have transformed but nothing has changed for my love. Princess Preziosa, will you marry me?

PREZIOSA
Oh, your highness, nothing would make me happier!

(They kiss. The queen wipes a tear from her eye.)

ANDREA
Well, that worked out much better than I expected.

QUEEN ANTONELLA
Anytime your desire satisfies your duty, it's a bit like magic. Come, Andrea. Let us give them their moment.

(They exit)

PREZIOSA
I didn't know I could be this happy! I'm delirious from joy!

PRINCE CIENZO
So I am, my love, but don't let it worry you. Love, it turns out, is the very best kind of madness.

End of play

Also by Hillary DePiano

HillaryDePiano.com

Full Length Plays

The Love of Three Oranges
comedy / fantasy /commedia dell'arte
90 to 120 minutes, 8 f, 8 m, 5 any (13-40+ actors possible: 7-20 f, 5-20 m)
A prince is cursed to fall in love with three magical oranges.

The Green Bird
comedy / fantasy /commedia dell'arte
90 to 120 minutes, 4 m 6 f 3 any (13-40+ actors possible)
Four royals, two clowns, and way too many talking statues must unravel the mystery of the green bird before an evil queen destroys the kingdom.

The Servant of 123 Masters
comedy / fantasy /commedia dell'arte
60 minutes (11-12 actors possible)
a hilarious parody of Sesame Street by way of Carlo Goldoni's The Servant of Two Masters

The Montholouges
contemporary / comedy / drama
30 to 70 minutes, 1 m 1 f 14 any (1-16 actors possible)
A funny, touching monologue play about all the ways who we are intersects with when we are.

One Act Plays

Week Daze
comedy
45 to 60 minutes, 6-7 any
Week Daze zooms out and looks at our daily routines from a new perspective as all five weekdays play out simultaneously across the stage in a comic ballet.

The Love of Three Oranges (One Act Version)
comedy / fantasy /commedia dell'arte
35 to 40 minutes, 8 f, 6 m, 4 any (10-30+ actors possible)
A prince is cursed to fall in love with three magical oranges.

The Green Bird (One Act Version)
comedy / fantasy /commedia dell'arte
35 to 45 minutes, 4 m 6 f 3 any (12-40+ actors possible)
Four royals, two clowns, and way too many talking statues must unravel the mystery of the green bird before an evil queen destroys the kingdom.

Nana's Happy Happy Good News Only Birthday Video Chat
comedy / streaming / contemporary
30 to 40 minutes, 5 m, 5 f (7-10 performers possible, flexible genders)
When a storm ruins the family's plans, Nana's grandkids organize a birthday video chat! But can this group of disasters pretend they've got their act together, or will life have other plans?

Daddy Issues
drama
15 to 20 minutes, 1 female, 1 male, 3 any
A young woman must confront the ghost of her past.

Polar Twilight
comedy / holiday
20 to 25 minutes, 3 f, 3 m (6 actors possible: 0-5 f, 1-6 m)
Everything you know about Santa is wrong and the truth kind of... sucks. Vampire Santa Claus... but in a cute way!

New Year's Thieve
comedy / holiday
30 to 35 minutes, 2 m 3 f 3 any (7 to 10+ actors possible)
Someone's stolen the New Year and the main suspect is... Frosty the coat rack?

SHORT PLAYS (10-15 MINUTES)

The Raven / Lenore

The Three Little Pigs and the Big Bad Storm

The (Completely Inaccurate) Legend of the Mummy Witch House

The Complete Novels of Jane Austen: Now New and Improved!

THREE PADDED WALLS

MASKS

NON-FICTION

BUILDING A WRITING LIFE
Do you want to write but have no idea where to begin? Building a Writing Life is the beginner writer's guide you've been looking for!

MAKE READY TO WRITE!
From novels and scripts to memoirs and more, your ultimate guide to prepping for a major writing project!

NANO WHAT NOW?
Finding your editing process, revising your NaNoWriMo book and building a writing career through publishing and beyond.

~

WRITING AS T. W. SELLER
THEWHINESELLER.COM

SELL THEIR STUFF
From eBay Trading Assistants to multichannel seller assistance, your ultimate guide to consignment selling online as a part-time income or full-time business

EBAY MARKETING MAKEOVER
Increase sales and grow traffic to your eBay items by encouraging word of mouth, focusing on your ideal buyers, and optimizing your selling for search and mobile

BEYOND AMAZON, EBAY, AND ETSY
Free and low cost alternative marketplaces, shopping cart solutions and e-commerce storefronts

About the Author

Hillary DePiano is a playwright, fiction and non-fiction author best known for fantastically funny fairy tales, surprisingly sweet slapstick and unrelentingly upbeat writing advice. With over two dozen plays for everyone from pre-schoolers and up, she's been honored to have her work performed in schools and theatres around the world.

A consummate cheerleader for writers at every experience level, Hillary teaches a variety of workshops and writing classes on everything from storycraft to marketing and beyond. She also teaches eBay, e-commerce and selling online under the name T. W. Seller (TheWhineSeller.com).

For more information about her books, plays, and blogs or for the schedule of upcoming events and workshops, visit HillaryDePiano.com.